Differences Found ⊘1 ⊘2 ⊘3 ○4 ⊘5 ○6 ○7 ○8 ○9 ○10

please leave us your feedback about the book

Please spare us a few minutes and leave us a rating and review on Amazon. We eagerly read all of your thoughtful comments because you are the one who help us to grow.

Thank you for your trust. We are grateful for your purchase. You can email your opinion, suggestion at *vivgamerinfo@gmail.com*

Differences Found ○1 ○2 ○3 ○4 ○5 ○6 ○7 ○8 ○9 ○10

Differences Found ○1 ○2 ○3 ○4 ○5 ○6 ○7 ○8 ○9 ○10

Differences Found ○1 ○2 ○3 ○4 ○5 ○6 ○7 ○8 ○9 ○10

Differences Found ○1 ○2 ○3 ○4 ○5 ○6 ○7 ○8 ○9 ○10

Differences Found ○1 ○2 ○3 ○4 ○5 ○6 ○7 ○8 ○9 ○10

Differences Found ○1 ○2 ○3 ○4 ○5 ○6 ○7 ○8 ○9 ○10

Differences Found ○1 ○2 ○3 ○4 ○5 ○6 ○7 ○8 ○9 ○10

Differences Found ○1 ○2 ○3 ○4 ○5 ○6 ○7 ○8 ○9 ○10

Differences Found ○1　○2　○3　○4　○5　○6　○7　○8　○9　○10

Differences Found ○1 ○2 ○3 ○4 ○5 ○6 ○7 ○8 ○9 ○10

GARDENING SUPPLIES

Differences Found ○1 ○2 ○3 ○4 ○5 ○6 ○7 ○8 ○9 ○10

Differences Found ○1 ○2 ○3 ○4 ○5 ○6 ○7 ○8 ○9 ○10

Differences Found ○1 ○2 ○3 ○4 ○5 ○6 ○7 ○8 ○9 ○10

HAPPY FAMILY ENJOYING WHILE PICKING APPLES

Differences Found ○1 ○2 ○3 ○4 ○5 ○6 ○7 ○8 ○9 ○10

Differences Found ○1 ○2 ○3 ○4 ○5 ○6 ○7 ○8 ○9 ○10

Differences Found ○1 ○2 ○3 ○4 ○5 ○6 ○7 ○8 ○9 ○10

Differences Found ○1 ○2 ○3 ○4 ○5 ○6 ○7 ○8 ○9 ○10

Differences Found ○1 ○2 ○3 ○4 ○5 ○6 ○7 ○8 ○9 ○10

Differences Found ○1 ○2 ○3 ○4 ○5 ○6 ○7 ○8 ○9 ○10

Differences Found ○1 ○2 ○3 ○4 ○5 ○6 ○7 ○8 ○9 ○10

Differences Found ○1 ○2 ○3 ○4 ○5 ○6 ○7 ○8 ○9 ○10

Differences Found ○1 ○2 ○3 ○4 ○5 ○6 ○7 ○8 ○9 ○10

Differences Found ○1 ○2 ○3 ○4 ○5 ○6 ○7 ○8 ○9 ○10

Differences Found ○1 ○2 ○3 ○4 ○5 ○6 ○7 ○8 ○9 ○10

Differences Found ○1 ○2 ○3 ○4 ○5 ○6 ○7 ○8 ○9 ○10

Differences Found ○1 ○2 ○3 ○4 ○5 ○6 ○7 ○8 ○9 ○10

Differences Found ○1 ○2 ○3 ○4 ○5 ○6 ○7 ○8 ○9 ○10

Differences Found ○1 ○2 ○3 ○4 ○5 ○6 ○7 ○8 ○9 ○10

SPRAY WATERING IN HYDRANGEA

Differences Found ○1 ○2 ○3 ○4 ○5 ○6 ○7 ○8 ○9 ○10

Differences Found ○1 ○2 ○3 ○4 ○5 ○6 ○7 ○8 ○9 ○10

Differences Found ○1 ○2 ○3 ○4 ○5 ○6 ○7 ○8 ○9 ○10

Differences Found ○1 ○2 ○3 ○4 ○5 ○6 ○7 ○8 ○9 ○10

Differences Found ○1 ○2 ○3 ○4 ○5 ○6 ○7 ○8 ○9 ○10

Differences Found ○1 ○2 ○3 ○4 ○5 ○6 ○7 ○8 ○9 ○10

Answer Sheet

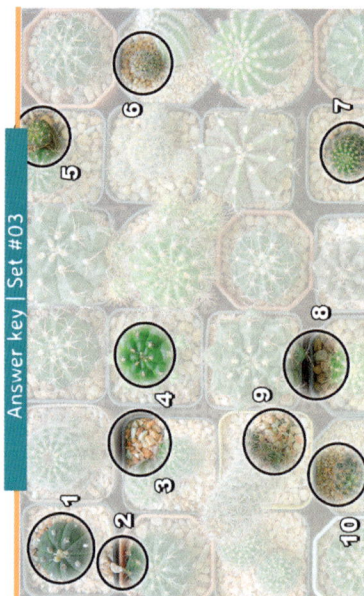

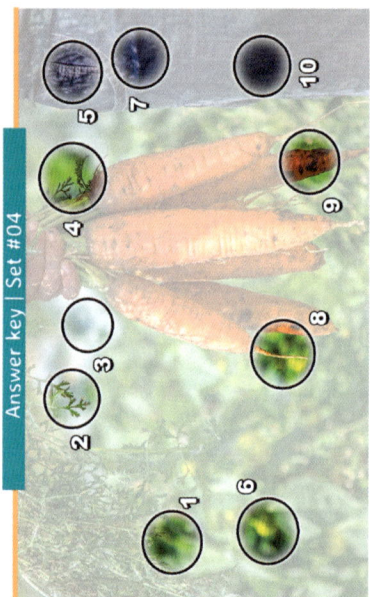

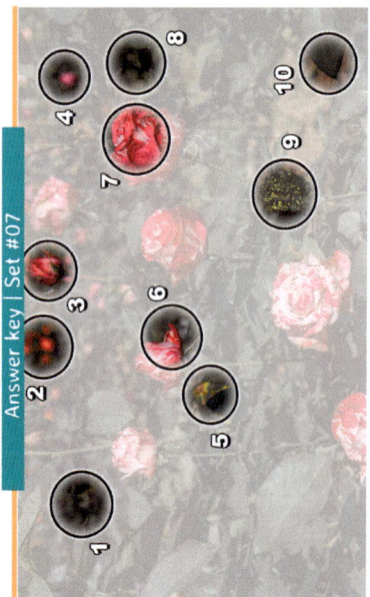

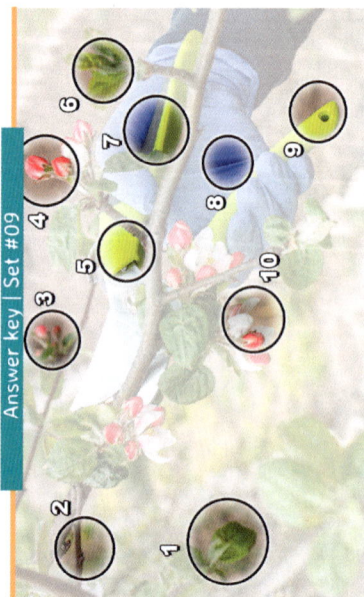

Answer Sheet

Answer key | Set #10

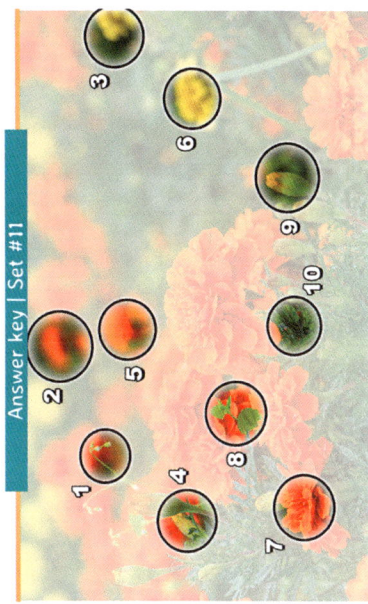

Answer key | Set #11

Answer key | Set #12

Answer key | Set #13

Answer key | Set #14

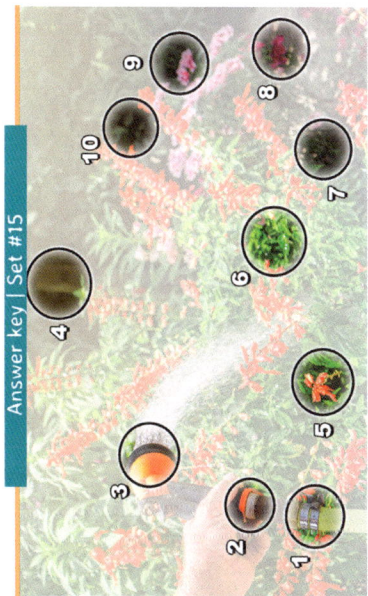

Answer key | Set #15

Answer key | Set #16

Answer key | Set #17

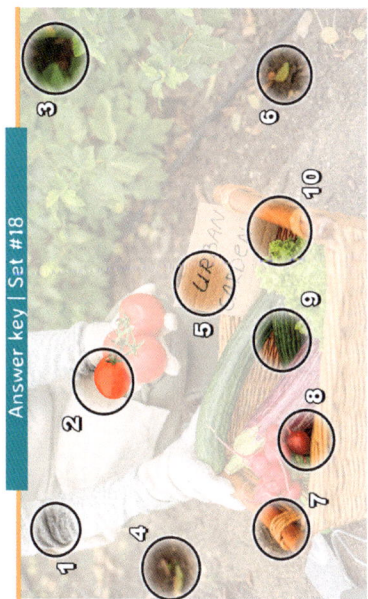

Answer key | Set #18

Answer Sheet

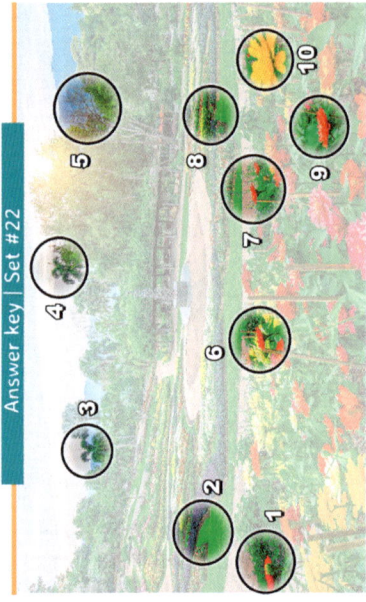

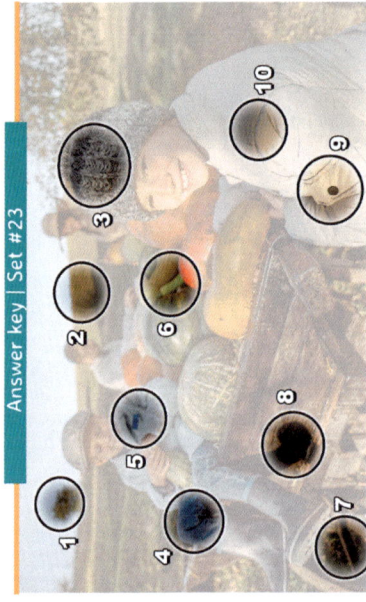

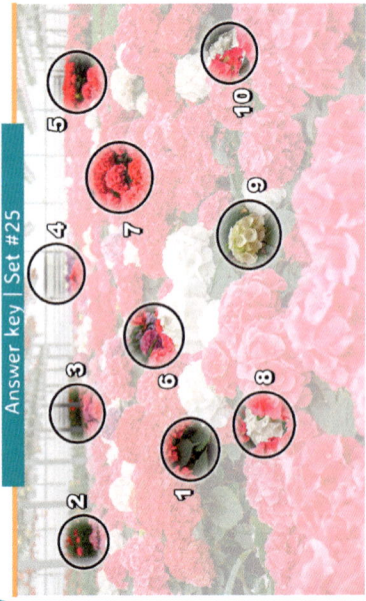

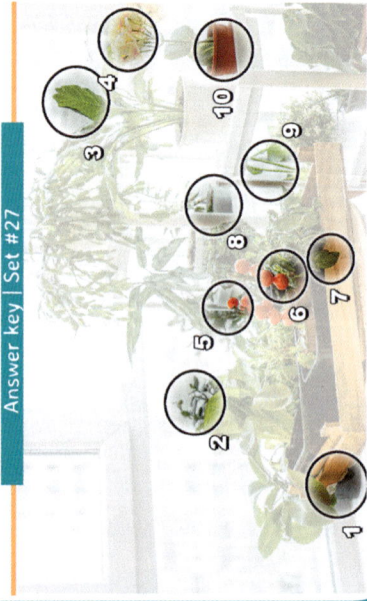

Answer key | Set #19

Answer key | Set #20

Answer key | Set #21

Answer key | Set #22

Answer key | Set #23

Answer key | Set #24

Answer key | Set #25

Answer key | Set #26

Answer key | Set #27

Answer Sheet

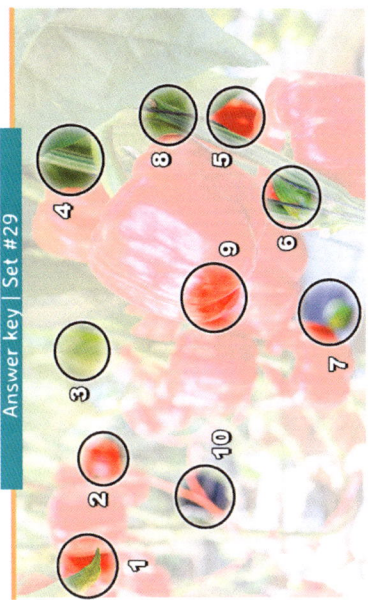

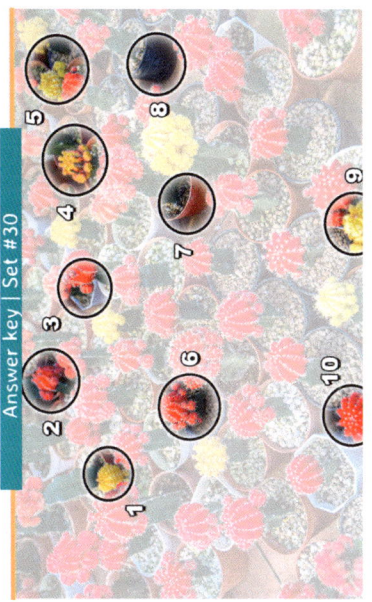

Answer Sheet

Answer key | Set #37

Answer key | Set #38

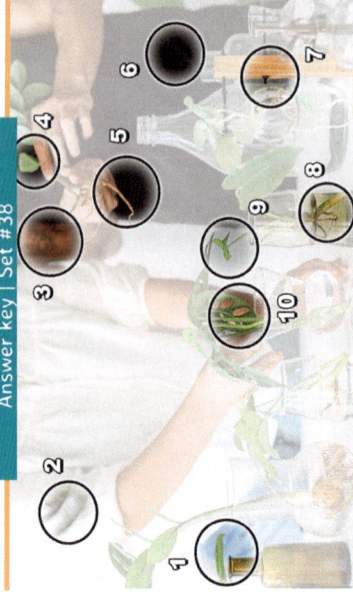

Answer key | Set #39

Answer key | Set #40

Printed in Great Britain
by Amazon